Poems about...

How could you know?

Poems about love

How could you know?

David Roberts

ACRIMONIOUS

For Julie

Poems about love

ISBN: 9798368341989

ACRIMONIOUS

Bishops Close, Hurstpierpoint,

BN6 9XU West Sussex UK

Website: davidrobertsblog.com

Cover photograph

Photographer Engin Akyurt, Pixabay Photo Library.

Contents

The Lyrics

Introduction

Love? What's it all about?

Since I first fell in love at the age of five and my parents came to blows when I was at junior school I've been very interested in love and human relationships. I don't think I'm unusual in this. Most of the world is interested in the personal relationships of others. Plays, films, books, the telly, the papers, and songs are full of romantic happenings, the triumphs and the tragedies of love. It's the stuff of gossip.

I think of many of my poems as "poetry of ideas" - based on observation, speculation, and, to a small extent, experience. Some poems are serious. Others are imaginative, surreal, bizarre, facetious.

This is not a normal book of love poetry. It goes beyond expressions of adoration, wonder, longing, and loss - the rhetoric of love poetry. It is a wide ranging exploration of "love" without being a comprehensive or a balanced book.

Love, like food, is essential for human survival but when either goes bad then it can become poisonous and even lethal. I'm interested in this aspect of love, too. It seems the ancient Greeks were aware that at least one kind of love can turn negative.

I've written as a white male, born in England during the second world war and brought up in a small village in Lincolnshire where my family, nominally Methodist Christians, had few social contacts. I went to an all-boys junior school and an all-boys grammar school - a sheltered and narrow upbringing. I left home at seventeen to work in London. After six years in commerce in London and Nottingham I became a student in Brighton. Then I moved into the neighbouring area of the county of Sussex where I have lived ever since. I taught in a comprehensive school for twenty-four years. I've been a publisher for a similar length of time and married for over fifty years.

I am therefore aware that my background, views and attitudes are not shared by many communities within our culturally and religiously diverse country and the wider world. Many communities live by rules and guidance which seek to restrict and safeguard personal relationships. Such ideas may not be found in my poems where degrees of freedom, instability and perhaps a casual attitude may be implied. Nevertheless, I think that many of my poems are true to life as I have observed it. Love happens. It is a vital element in every society and every life, however much communities may try to control it.

I've used the word "love" in this introduction and in the poems without defining it. Part of the idea of bringing these poems together was to present them as an exploration of love and the wider nature of love. What I was mainly writing about was sexual desire and attraction, or feelings of affection and the impulse to care for someone, or a combination of these - behaviour that is particularly associated with short or long-term relationships or a bond between two people, and is the idea of love that is commonly the subject of love poetry.

The ancient Greeks, over two thousand years ago, had at least six words to describe different kinds of love. It's interesting to use their ideas as a guide to the topic and contrast their wider understanding of love with my informal look at it.

Six kinds of love according to the ancient Greeks

First, "agape". This term refers to unconditional love like the love felt for one's children and which Christians use to describe the love of God for his children and the love of Christians for God. Agape also covers charitable feelings and desiring the well-being of others.

Second, "eros". This is sexual desire and appreciation of the physical form and experience of the one desired.

Third, "philia". This is true friendship, usually between equals, and loyalty to friends, family and community.

Fourth, "storge". This has been described as common empathy, identifying with others. Admiration of others such as a favourite sports team, a famous person, one's country, etc.

Fifth, "philautia". This is self-love and has good and bad possibilities. When it is good it is self-respect, appreciation of one's abilities and qualities, concern for one's own well-being or advantage. The bad or unhealthy form of self love is an obsession with one's self, vanity, arrogance, selfishness.

Sixth, "xenia". Hospitality, kindness to strangers, respect for strangers, generosity. The ancient Greeks regarded xenia as a civic duty.

So love takes many forms, and feelings of love in all its forms, not just between two people, enable the fruitful functioning of civilised societies. Even so, love has not proved to be the answer to every personal and social problem, nor to all the world's great challenges and conflicts. Perhaps love is a too unreliable human characteristic. Maybe there is too little love and goodwill around to do what is needed.

It is evident in life and some of my poems that there is a wild, even uncontrollable, element in human behaviour.

I hope that in my collection of poems and epigrams about love, in straying from the conventional in love poetry, I have captured something of a wider and more varied experience of love.

Note

In writing some of the following pieces I was thinking of some of them as suitable for singing rather than reading - lyrics, rather than poems.

The Poems

Love is its own reward

Some people stand apart,
have no need of status,
recognition,
or the world's approval.
They have risen
above the need for love or lovers
because they have it all
within themselves and love to spare
and give it all to others.

5 December 2022

You are

You are
my every day surprise,
the sunshine in my eyes,
the only fish in the sea,
the catch of the day,
the site of my life,
my every spring,
my fuschia,
my all.

19 July 1968

The last train

All things must change.
Sunshine turns to rain.
Lovers become estranged.

Tonight I think
the final kiss.

I didn't want it
to end like this.

You've changed.
You didn't explain.

You didn't confess.
Perhaps I can guess.

What do I care?
But I do care.

I step out
into the rain.

Empty streets,
empty heart.

I feel
that too familiar pain

and tears
on my cheeks.

I can feel
my heart beat.

Just time
to catch the last train.

All things must change.
Sunshine turns to rain.
Lovers become estranged.

10 July 2007, 25 August 2016, 2 January 2019

Does love exist?

Love was first described
in ancient texts
written by nomadic tribes.
Now people question whether
we can place reliance
on the writing
of such elementary scribes.

So! To the big question:
love, does it exist?

First we must define the word
and say exactly what is meant.
Only then can science
play its part,
investigate,
gather evidence.

Can this entity be quantified?
What are
its physical characteristics?
What data has been gathered?
Scientists can't simply trust

the word of mystics.
Is it a gas? A liquid?
Or solid matter that we can see?
Is it a force
that can move an object
from A to B?
Is it an organism
that can be cultivated or observed?

No evidence
has been presented.
Love is none of these.
The concept is absurd.

Yet, today,
people say
belief in love
is almost universal,
but scientists are not impressed.
For centuries, they say,
the whole world believed
that the earth was flat.
But now this myth has been exploded.
Everyone knows
that this is NOT a fact!

Belief is not scientific evidence.

Belief is not the same as science.
Love, one may speculate
is a kind of myth,
or a hope, or a wish
or a collective delusion
that one finds
in heated imaginations
or in simple minds.

One well-respected scientist
has written a famous book,
"The Love Delusion",
and by carefully applying
scientific rules
proved
that love does not exist
and that lovers
are just deluded fools.

However,
not all scientists agree.
Some scientists now believe
that love began
with a big bang
deep in outer space
which actually explains
the origin of the human race -

a phenomenon
astonishingly complex,
with,
at its heart,
the motivating force
of love and sex.

1 October 2021

50 Kinds of Love

Love needs no introduction
Love needs no introduction,
it's everywhere.
The human race lives by love,
but it's little understood,
so, to add to the confusion and chatter
this is just
a collection of observations and examples
of love's endless formulations:
a kaleidoscope of mysteries
perplexities, triumphs, necessities,
illusions and obituaries.
Something to think about.
Something to add to.
This is incomplete.
Read it,
then over to you.

Instant love
Love,
when electricity flows
and lights light up
and fuses sizzle

and fireworks pop.
Love at first sight
Love at first night.
Love at first bite.

Holiday romance.
Love at first chance.

Fragile love
Love that's meant but not spoken.
Love that's spoken but not meant.
Love that was perfect
that's now broken.
Love that will not pay the rent.
Love that was rich,
but is now spent.

Imagined love
Some dream of love,
the trampoline of love.

Love on the rebound.

Love that hesitates.
Love that vacillates.
Love that will not commit
and isn't really it.

Away-with-the-fairies love.

Heavens-above! Love.

Doubtful love
Love
that doesn't know the meaning of.
Love that's just a dream
in your head
and will never
see you in bed.

Stay-at-home love,
living in the hope of love.

Love that's paper thin,
just a whim.

Unrequited love
that's not quite love.

"I'm-sorry-I-don't-remember-you," love.

I've-searched-the-world-over-and never-found-it love.
Never-quite-good-enough love.
Any-love-is good-enough love.
More-or-less love.

Faithless love.
Hopeless love.
Worthless love.
Love that's a tangled mess.

The counterfeit of love
Love
that takes you for a ride.
Love on the make.
Love that fakes.
Love that runs away,
and does not want
to face the light of day.

Trophy love.
Atrophied love.

Unexpected love
Love that finds you,
magnifies you.
Love that finds a way.

Love against the odds
Love that cannot be explained
at all
but lasts though nations fall.

Love lost

Love that
hesitates,
procrastinates,
until it is too late.

The best love

Love that's the best you've ever had.
Love that's the best you're gonna get.
Love not to be missed.
Love in a mist.

The persistence of love

Love that cannot wait.
Love that will not go away.
Love that is here to stay.

Wicked love

Love that is stolen
and is now possessed
and no-one else matters.
One world lights up.
Another world shatters.

Love that risks the wildest seas.
Love that cries and almost bleeds.

Incendiary love

Love that's a rumble of thunder.

Love that's a flash of lightning.

Love that plays with fire

and burns the whole house down.

Dangerously risky love

Secret love,

discreet love,

be-careful-where-you-meet love.

Love that must be kept under wraps.

Love in the balance

that may succeed,

perhaps.

Love on the side.

Love on the other side.

Time-share love

Love in distant towns.

Love out of bounds.

Love on the up

Love that

permeates

fascinates

illuminates

educates

reciprocates.

Love that builds.

Love that fulfils.

The highs and lows of love

Love without a care.

Love in the fresh air.

Love where the grass is greener.

Love in pastures new.

Love where the air is cleaner.

Love where the sky is blue.

Love at the crossroads.

Love that's an uphill struggle.

Love that's on the way up!

Love on a mountain top.

Love on a slippery slope.

Love that's downhill from now on.

Love that's without hope,

though hope lingers on.

Love

that's the end of the road.

True love
Love that
appreciates
celebrates
co-operates.

Love that is
caring
sharing
daring.

Can this be love?
That's-all-right-I-can-find-someone-else love.
There-are-plenty-more-lovers-in-the-sea, love.

Basic love
Good, old-fashioned, you-and-me love.
Sensual love.
Consensual love.
Delighted
in being united.

Geometric love
Straight love.
Bent love.
Zigzag love.

Numerical love

Love of many.

Love of few.

Love of just one.

Love of just two.

Love that adds up.

Love that multiplies.

Love that is a difficult equation:

insoluble, incalculable, unfathomable.

Love in different directions

Love that's straight as an arrow.

Love that crisscrosses.

Love that double crosses.

Degrees of love

Platonic love.

Supersonic love.

Gin and tonic love.

Moronic love.

Mindless love.

Intellectual love.

Spiritual love.

Mind, body and soul love.

Love that's profound.

Love with your head in the clouds.

Love with your feet on the ground.

Exclusive love

Love that's possessive

and aggressive.

Love that passeth understanding.

Young love

Love without a care.

Love without caution.

Love without commitment.

Love without a risk assessment.

Contrasting loves

Hot love: cold love.

Shy love: bold love.

New love: old love.

Free love: sold love.

Sincere love: cavalier love.

Love that is salvation:

love that is damnation.

Love that swerves.

Love that deserves.

Summer games of love

Love that starts the balls rolling.

Love that bowls you over.

Love in fields of clover.

Love that's not cricket.

Love that bowls you out.

Thoughts of love

Love of naked girls in magazines.

Love of films with sexy scenes.

Love of carrots,

as well as greens.

Objects of desire

Love of a beef-cake.

Love of a sweetie-pie.

Love of a pussy-cat.

Love of a rattle snake

Love of a heartless rat.

Love of a battleship.

Difficult Love

Pernickety love

that makes love rickety.

Love that's poetic.

Love that's chaotic.

Love that's logistically impossible.
Love that's difficult to rhyme.

Inappropriate behaviour love.
Mutual inappropriate behaviour love.

Love that takes up all your time.

Sensations of love
Love in a storm.
Love in the stillness of dawn.
Love that keeps you safe from harm.
Love that keeps you warm.

Love that is a ballet.
Love that is a rally.
Love that is love all.

Love that is good for your ego.
Love in a cheap hotel.
Love in a gazebo.
Love in the winter snow.

Recreational love.
Procreational love.

Love with intent.
Love in a tent.

Sustainable love
with the heat turned down low.

Love at your finger tips.
Love on the tip of your tongue.

The start and end of love
Cold-calling love.
Love that is a slow burn.
Love that is a no burn.
Love that burns the candle at both ends.
Love that is burnt out.

Nascent love - how does love begin?
A look, a glance,
a thought, a dance,
some words, a chance. . ?
OR
an observation,
a casual conversation,
a growing realisation,
unexpected animation,
then, perhaps, an invitation . . ?
OR
attraction, reaction,
interaction, connection,

fascination, inspiration,

sensation, admiration,

cooperation

and,

maybe,

procreation.

OR

Nowadays

the internet beckons.

Sign up online:

forty replies

in 0.34 seconds.

OR

Love that asks,

love that invites.

Love that phones.

Love that writes.

Fractious love

Cat and dog love.

Cat and mouse love.

Dog in a manger love.

The love of dogs, cats, mice, and mangers.

Love where the eyes have it.

The eyes have it.

The hooks and eyes of love.
The looks and lies of love.

Love, when even in bed you lie.

Action-packed love
Love that's
vociferous, splendiferous,
tit-for-tat, tat-for-tit,
on your guard
no holds barred,
ding-dong love.
Gloves off love.
Everything off love.
Head over heels love.
Acrobatic love.
Lusty, busty, rusty, dusty love.
Absolutely all over you love.

It's all over, love.

Magic love
Oh, the love by candle-light.
Oh, the stroke of midnight!
So beautiful in the night
and in the light of dawn
more beautiful.

Unbalanced love

The need-to-be-loved love
that's unequal to the task of love.
Love that hasn't got its head screwed on.
Weak and needy love.
Love that's just plain wrong.

The I-love-you-so-much-why-don't-you-love-me love.
Love that cannot handle love.
Love that's out of control.
Love that's a sticking plaster.
Love that's a disaster.
Love that's an own goal.

Love that moves too fast

Love that moves too fast
and shows its hand too early
and put its foot in it,
and is, perhaps, a step too far,
or maybe just a slip of the tongue.

Light touch love

Occasionally together love
that's light touch, light hearted,
smiling, delighted,
that doesn't ask too much,
is pleased and contented.

Problem love

Jealous love.

Rejected love.

Dangerous love.

Taboo love.

Criminal love.

Abused love.

Arranged love.

Externally controlled love.

Forbidden love.

Hidden love.

Love that disrupts.

This-will-stress-our-children love.

Love that deserves love

Love that is patient and respects

and is kind, true, generous and loyal.

Love that connects.

Love?

I-must be-home-before-midnight love.

This-will-upset-your-parents love.

It-seemed-a-good-idea-at-the-time love.

Let's-keep-it-a-secret love.

I-suppose-we'd-better-go-public love.

Don't-tell-your-wife/husband love.

I-don't-care-what-people-think love.
Let's-get-the-press-onto-this love.
Let's-have-a-big-family love.
Let's-have-no-children love.
We-don't-need-to-get-married love.
Only-when-we-are-married love.
We-can't-predict-the-future love.
This-is-not-the-most-important-thing-in-my-life love.

The love of . . .
The love of dogs.
The love of cats.
The love of women
who are bats.

Quick love
Quick and free and casual love.
Love with no buttons and no strings.

Attic love
Love in an attic.
Love that's aromatic.
Love that's ecstatic.
Love that's problematic.
Love that's pragmatic.
Love that's dramatic.
Love that's always at it.

Placeholder love

Love till the right one comes along.

The shelf-life of love

Love that is "long-life" love.

Love that is "best before" love.

Love that is out of date.

Vintage love.

Love that has aged well.

Love that has aged badly.

Love that has gone off.

That-was-then-and-this-is-now love.

Love that changes

Love, that once it's awake

finds it was a mistake

and evaporates.

Love

that over time

finds the lover changed

so nothing is the same.

Then the questioning,

the disbelief, the pain.

Love destroyed by outside forces

Sincere love that's hit by storms and shipwreck –
business failure, financial ruin, career disaster, alcohol –
humiliation, overwhelming stress, emotional collapse –
the death of love.

Heartbreak

There is heartbreak at the heart of love.
After the happiness of all the years
comes the loss,
the emptiness,
the tears.

Love that lasts

Love till the last breath.
Love beyond death.

Love timed out

Love, when one of you says,
like life itself,
I'm really sorry, but I can't stay long.
The song was great,
but it was just a song.

Fifty kinds of love was written, a fragment at a time, from August
2013 to December 2022.

In the beginning

In the beginning, male and female created he them,

with different,

but complementary,

genitalia.

Had he not done so, then procreation would have been a failure.

Into each Jack and Jill he placed the illusion of free will.

Into Eve he planted the desire to conceive.

Into Adam's book

he wrote an incessant desire to

do DIY and put up shelves, and perform almost any other kind of action,

as a distraction, in a mind that was NOT complex

and could otherwise only think of sex.

And so, with lovely Eve, Adam had many years of fun.

They had loads of kids. They did not plan.

And that was how the human race began.

And it came to pass, in the fullness of time,

that human beings out-rabbited rabbits,

and over-populated the planet.

And now, some people, as they consider the species
which, as a whole,
has the morality of gannets and is so clearly oversexed,
are asking a very serious question:
what next?

26 December 2012

The Diplodocus

The ludicrous diplodocus
I used to laugh
at the diplodocus.
He had two brains
so just couldn't focus.

One brain in his head,
one brain in his tail,
with an arrangement like that
he was set up to fail.

How could he decide
what to do next
when one brain said eat
and the other said sex?

So people laugh
at the diplodocus
though the creature couldn't help it,
didn't know what the joke was.

The clever humans
Today, I sat, sipping coffee
in a cafeteria,

and mused on the brilliance
of the human race
and how the poor diplodocus
was inferior.

We humans believe
that the human race
sits on top
of the evolutionary tree.
We are it,
the tops, the best,
the clever, the wise.
We've won first prize.

We
have free will.
The world is ours
and all that's in it
to use and exploit
or to waste
and to bin it.

We
are the rulers of earth
and heaven,
the chosen creatures
of God.

So how odd
that just like the diplodocus   [short o]
we are prone
to similar cock-ups.

Human imperfection
And the reason for this
is plain.
We also have
a second brain -
elusive, invisible, a force like the mind,
a button, a spot, a twinge, or an ache;
a pleasure, a plaything, a treasure?
A curse? A mistake?

Hard to identify,
difficult to place,
the source of desire,
The source of temptation,
the source of our daring,
the source of our urges, emotions and instincts.
When our free-will goes missing
we do what it thinks.

It's the brain twixt our limbs,
the brain in our crotch,

a lesser brain, a lower brain,
a brain with no name.

The lower brain and the young and immature
This lesser brain,
the brain with no brain,
is a gift
to each maturing girl and boy,
a pack of urges, fearless and thoughtless
offering danger, disaster,
fun, excitement, joy.

This lesser brain,
may stay in charge
for many years,
break all the rules,
wreck the world,
leave people reeling,
hurt, shocked,
in distress.
The lower brain
creates headlines,
creates a mess.

The upper brain
But the upper brain
can see the future

and the bigger picture,
plans ahead,
understands consequences,
is moral,
follows rules,
shows compassion,
is no fool.

The lower brain
The lower brain
is the spanner in the works,
the dissenting voice,
fearless and unpredictable
but full of energy,
full of force.

The lower brain delights in:
deviation from the social norm,
the novel, the new,
the dangerous, the fun,
pleasure-seeking,
pretending what is false is true,
shunning responsibility,
going on the run.

The lower brain
feels no guilt, no shame.

The lower brain
is inclined
to dream, to fantasize
to be passionate, or indifferent,
ruthless or blasé,
be brief in grief,
unhinged, unwise.

But there is a bright side
to the lower brain.
Within its turmoil
are qualities much prized:
the creative, the adventurous,
the inventive, the visionary -
behold
the seeds of progress,
love and games,
the seeds of change.

But the lower brain
can turn deadly black.
If the dark side
ascends the throne,
beware.
Enter the extortionist,
the exhibitionist, the fighter, the destroyer,
cruel, terrifying, insidious,

manipulative, adversarial,
venomous, dictatorial,
power obsessed,
possessed -
a brain
that's insane.

The brains in conflict
Within each creature
human and diplodocan
was always a tension,
conflicting voices,
two directions,
two choices.

As with individuals
so with the state,
in the flocks and the herds,
one voice would dominate.

Diplodocan survival
For aeons
the diplodocan leaders
were possessed of foresight.
Their followers were
an upper-brained flock

resisting the urges
of the lower brain
always snapping at its back.

When a human funks the challenge
So, just like a diplodocan,
a man may be guided
by his upper brain,
whilst unseen and everywhere
like pollen in the air,
scents, signals, magnetic forces,
enticing invitations, beguiling voices
build him up
to bring him down.

He may have led
a steady and a blameless life,
have three children
and a loving wife,
be balanced, rational, controlled, refined,
a model citizen, admired,
respected, kind:

till, one day,
BAM!
Stunning attraction

like an electric shock!
Love finds him.
Love unintended,
love unforeseen,
love overpowering,
love extreme.

He is helplessly entangled,
his steady life mangled,
as he writhes
on the rusty pin of fate
he will struggle in vain,
a victim of his lesser brain.

His family and friends
are in disbelief.
His shame
is fanfared in the press.
His emotions
are in turmoil -
so much elation,
so much stress.

Brains for survival
So, you see,
the two brains are rarely matched
in people and in flocks.

Fortunately, for diplodocus,
the upper brain, the one in his head,
(the good, the wise, that could plan ahead)
dominated the diplodocan race
for thousands of years,
so, in spite of many attacks
from many a rival
the diplodocus
ensured survival.

The battle of the brains
But then came deviants
with lower brains that were oversized,
reckless, thrusting, prolific and dangerous,
changing the settled order,
rushing to modernise,
unable to read the future,
the consequences of their actions
immune to common sense and good advice.

Finale
They replaced the counsels of the wise
with raucous battle cries
taking chances
risking territorial advances.
Confident in the power of flashier teeth

and sharper incisors
they led their diplodocan armies
till defeated
and all their lands
and all reserves depleted.

They took their fellows to the brink,
but worse than that,
they became extinct.

So how like us,
the diplodocus?

5 August 2022

Out of Love

There are those who want no love,
are outside of love,
have given up on love,
don't understand love,
are too shy for love,
would rather die than love,
dare not take the risk of love,
have no hope of love,
and are content
to have no love.

Some,
alone,
After a lifetime of love and loss,
look no more for love.

But there are some,
who feel excluded from love,
and,
loveless,
cry for love.

October 2021

Anti-love Love

There are some
who have known no love,
feel no love,
feel no need of love,
are hardened against love.

Loveless, they hate love,
and in their jealousy
or numb incomprehension
hate the loving,
and turn to abuse
and domination
and destruction
and love hate
and violence
and conflict,
and cruelty
and power
and pain.

1 October 2021, from notes 28 June 2020

Jigsaw loves

All pieces complete
The perfect picture.

Only the framing pieces so far found.
Pieces difficult to place.
Pieces missing, no trace.

A puzzle that is utter confusion
as pieces from two puzzles are mixed
to make a puzzle that can never be fixed.

A puzzle with
pieces that are tinged with guilt,
a puzzle that may never be built.

Love, a puzzle that is just too difficult.

2 October 2021

Where are the girls that once I loved?

Where are the girls
that once I loved?
And those I liked
but did not love,
who gave me hope
but disappointed,
and those that did not disappoint,
the ones I loved.

Sixty years or so ago,
a lifetime.
I can't pretend I've thought of you often,
but still,
You're not forgotten.
Not completely.

Where are the girls
that I half remember?
The girls of springtime
and sunshine
and winter nights,
the girls who smiled
and laughed and danced.

Girls shy, laid-back, aloof and whimsical,
cool and self-possessed,
ambiguously inviting, enticing.
Some, readily intoxicated,
sexy, exciting and irresponsible.
Girls with come-hither eyes -
unconsciously beguiling?
Or was it meant?
I found them irresistible.
Thither I went.

Girls let loose on the world
escapees,
beyond parental control.
wide-eyed young workers
and A-level lovers,
full of hope
and looking for love,
amazed at what the world offered,
ready to believe anything,
and really,
so naive.
We were all so ignorant and naive
but fired by divine inspiration
to practise for procreation.

Those were the days!

We were young
with all our lives before us.
Life was fun
and life was glorious.

Without thought for the future
it seemed this wonderful world
would last for ever.

Over a few years,
imperceptibly things changed.
We changed.
I changed.
Careless,
neglecting, then rejecting,
then rejected
I left town,
moved south to a different world
a different life,
and found a wife.

I admit
that when I moved
I received your letters,
but did not reply.
It seemed right to forget
the girls I'd loved.

Since then
sixty years have vanished.
So where are you now?
Who are you now?

You are other lives
I might have had.
I puzzle over what might have been.
There is no answer. We will never know.
I think you were better off without me, though.

So,
Life, how was it for you.
What have you become?
What did you do?
Has life been kind?
Is life still fun?
Are you rich or poor?
Do you live in style?
Or just get by?

Did you sink or swim?

In commerce?
In social services?
Academic?
A great success?
On benefit?

A leading authority on alternative energy?
Maybe still on top of your game,
speaking at conferences around the world,
at home with fame?
Someone important in the NHS?
A store manager for Tesco?
In admin for UNESCO?
Work on a check-out at M&S?

Can't possibly know.
All this is just a wild guess.

But some things are pretty certain.
I bet you all got married.
I hope to someone
dependable and true
who really took
good care of you.

Did your marriages last?
Maybe some.
Bereaved?
Deceived?
Did he leave you or you leave him?

Did your children find love?
Did they shine and prosper
and now live abroad?

Perhaps grandchildren
take up all your time?
If so, you're lucky there.

And how do you look?
Still good looking, I'm sure,
but sags and lines?
Your skin in decline?
Sadly there's no cure
for the advance of time.

Are you shorter, broader, rounder, fatter?
Or maybe thinner, slimmer, leaner, fitter?

Do you ride, swim, ski,
do zumba, pilates, yoga,
voluntary work,
t'ai chi,
play golf, badminton,
learn Spanish and Latin,
jive and Scottish dancing,
tutor children,
go to concerts,
sing in choirs,
have many friends,
and walk for miles?

How are you on stairs?
Do you walk with a stick?
Have you had
replacement hips?

Have you escaped
cancer, Parkinsons, arthritis,
heart attacks, strokes, diabetes?

How does it feel to be so old?
Are you still very bright,
full of vigour, smiling,
never been better?
Or are you in obvious decline,
your thoughts turning bitter,
losing your mind,
not knowing what day it is,
unable to tell the time?

Has your partner gone?
Are you living alone?
Are you in a home?

This year
five of my friends have died.
Are you still alive?

If you've gone,

it's all been too quick,

too neat.

Lives lived.

Lives complete.

A conjuror's vanishing trick.

We've done it. We've had it.

Game over. There's no going back.

Game over?

At our age,
if any of you are still alive,

we have the exit door in view.

I think I'm a long way from it.

How about you?

2014 – 2022

Love, what is it?

Is it instinct?
Is it reason?
Is it emotion?
Is it chemistry or magnetism?
Or empathy or alchemy?
Is it written in the stars
or shown in the eyes?
Is it smell and touch
and the voice and the looks?

Is it wishful thinking
or the meeting of minds
or the attraction of opposites?
Is it a revelation
or a realisation?

Can it be learned?
Can it be fostered?
Can it be crushed?
or abused or perverted?
or talked about too much?

June 2022

Love is

Love is a divine itch
looking for a scratch.

2010

Questions about love

Oh love, love, love!
Love, please tell me.

Can you find it
If you can't define it?

If you haven't got it,
Can you make it?

If you haven't got it,
can you fake it?

If you have it,
can you hide it?

Oh love, love, love!
Love, what is it?

1st October 2021

A heart in winter

Sense of sunlight
on my eyes

Open them
Room dark

No one
by my side

Violin
silent

Heart cries

Footsteps in the street

Love dies.

3 August 2002

Written after seeing the French film, *Un coeur en hiver*.

Heatwave

The hottest day recorded.
Towards ten at night
The rain started.

We walked out
Into the garden, naked,
enjoying the refreshing rain.

The lawn was squelchy
underfoot.

We lay down together,
and
made mud.

27th July 2019

Easy Love

Remember
the days
of easy love?

Remember
the days
when love was light?

Remember
the smiles
that lit your life?

What a time to be alive!
No cash,
no cares,
no fears,
no ties.
What a time to be alive!

Work was soft
and life
was pleasure.
Those were the days

that would last
for ever
when all was fresh
and we were
clever.

Remember
the days
of easy love?

Those were the days of easy love.
What a time to be alive!
What a time to be alive!

6 September 2017
On Ryanair flight to Palermo.

Never again

Never again such innocence.
Never again so coy.
All that blissful ignorance.
Never again such joy.

December 2014

Adeline

Ah, yes,
I remember Adeline
the first girl
I thought of
as mine.

Walking on a hill one day
with half a dozen friends
she appeared beside me
and walked close
and seemed to like me.
So I liked her.
She looked into my eyes.
What did this mean?
Enquiring?
Admiring?
Hoping?
Challenging?
Desiring?

Without thinking
as if a natural thing to do
I put my arm around her.
She smiled.

How nice!
She welcomed it.
She gave me a kiss.
Oh, Adeline!

In time
we grew together
as I began to explore
and learn much more
about her.

She liked to be touched.
She did not resist.
She liked to be kissed.

And we grew closer.

And so
for many months
a year or more
we enjoyed
an innocent kind of bliss,
pure pleasure
in being together.

Now
on reflection
it is clear

there was no depth
to our affection -
just the simple joy
of girl with boy.

6 January 2017

I is what I is

I is what I is.
You am
what you am.
But what is so special
is you is my man.

I is for you
and you is for me.
That's how it always been.
That's how it gonna be.

I lover you,
and you
lover me.
That's how it always been.
That's how it gonna be.

I lover you
cause you am
what you am.
I lover you
cause you is my man.

2 May 2022

Darling, the Flight

Flight delayed.
We wait.
The long anticipation!
My heart is racing.

At last
some stirrings in the cockpit.
Announcement: We have a slot.

We are moving,
taxying out to the runway
to our starting spot,
engines gently trembling
ready for the off.
A pause.

Again we are moving.
At first a slow acceleration.
then a surge of power
a sudden thrust,
the forward dash.
And in a moment
up we rise
and climb the summit of the skies.

I loved it.

I loved the take-off.

What a thrill!

And Oh!

The ride!

The bliss!

The onward glide!

I loved the feeling

of the flight.

The turbulence

was pure delight.

What a way

to spend the night!

Darling,

the flight

was wonderful.

3 April 2004

On a plane on a parking/boarding area for planes at Gatwick airport. Two hour flight delay. "Fog in Venice." Revised 28 December 2022

First Day at Uni, 2020

A poem in covid times

I remember that first day.
I saw you
two metres away.

We went for a walk
in the park
two metres apart.

If we had met in another time.
we could be together
but now must stay apart
for ever.

June 2020

Origin of *First Day at Uni* - a poetry competition for ten-line poems

For ten years the small town and port of Shoreham-by-Sea, on the south coast of England, just along the coast from Brighton, has had a thriving, popular literary festival. In the year 2000, the tenth anniversary of the festival, the organisers decided to run a poetry competition. The competition rules required a ten line poem on any subject.

First Day at Uni was one of my submissions. I thought it pointed up a very important issue: the serious deprivation being inflicted on young people by the social distancing laws brought in as a defence against the covid 19 virus.

I read that some universities were employing security firms to police and enforce social distancing on students. This seemed to me an outrageous idea.

So I was against social distancing for young people who were at little risk from the disease according to scientific evidence. For all of us social distancing goes against natural human behaviour. Logically, if adhered to, it would lead to the end of the human race. It must surely be against basic human rights. And there is much more one could say in criticism of it, but for young people the idea that they cannot come near each other struck me as preposterous.

Star attraction

This guy is hot.
Just what has he got?
What has he not?

He's arrived
and all over town
word's got around.

He's surrounded by masses
of girls in dark glasses.

Young mothers with prams
are creating traffic jams.
There are women with knives
and passionate wives
in 4-wheel drives.

These women pursue him.
What might they do to him?

Girls flutter eyelashes
and come out in rashes.
Birds fall from the trees.

Girls collapse at his knees.
They are biting
like fleas.
He's hounded
surrounded
dumbfounded.

Help!
He never wanted this.
Help him someone!
Call the police!

1 September 2007

Love in various positions

Cheating in love
"isn't cricket".
But if you play the game fairly
what are your favourite positions?

In the outfield?
At silly mid on,
at silly mid off,
in the slips,
at mid wicket?

How do you like it?
Long on,
long off,
long stop?

Have you tried
deep square leg,
or short fine leg?

Best to avoid
leg slip,
boot hill,
and a sticky wicket.

Have you thought of
the gully,
the rough,
or the square?

Or deep extra cover?
Maybe your safest bet.

You could have a session
in the nets.

How about
an away game or two?

Poor light
starts play?

Whatever you do
mind you don't get
caught behind.

21 June 2021

This wood

This wood's a fine
and private place,
just right, I think,
to here embrace.

23 Jan 2019

Tiny little animals

We're tiny little animals
cuddling in our nest,
floating in a universe,
like a speck of dust.

We haven't got much time
so be merry, eat and drink.
Our lives are quickly over.
They're gone just in a blink.

17 January 2019

Marriage

When push comes to shove
marriage is not about love.

And a wedding
is not "the happy ending".
It is the beginning
of a long journey
with a contract to travel for the rest of your life
with someone you hardly know
By a route and
towards a destination
that no-one knows.

2004 and 1 January 2023

Aegean Days

Early morning and the sun already warm,
we discover a deserted bay.

We swim.
We laze.
You sit on a rock
pensively moving your toes in the water.

I lie face down on the beach,
hot sun on my back,
the sand upholding me.
I hear no voices,
just the sea gently lapping,
the lazy splashing of the waves.
I am caressed by a soft warm breeze.

I am blessed to be alive
in this place
at this time.

I love days like these.

8 August 2002

A beach near Aliki, Thassos Island. In 2002 the beach
was deserted, timeless. Twenty years later it is a resort.

Every day I breathe

Every day I breathe
is a gift to me.
What more could I wish?
What more could I have?

I swim in warm seas.
The sun shines every day.
I walk the hills without a care.
I breathe the fresh air.

A loving family
I love.
What more could I wish!
What more could I have!

I know the sun will always shine.
The pleasures of the earth are mine.

15 August 2002
Thassos

Our love

Our love
which art on earth,
wonderful is thy name.
This bliss on earth
is really just like heaven
and long may it remain.

19 July 1968

More than any poem

A poem
is not music.
No poem can represent the sea.

A sad poem
can only be
less than the palest shadow
of melancholy.

No poem
can equal mountains.

No poem
can convey a flower
or a happy child.

No poem can mean
what our love means.
We are alive.
This is LIFE,
And more than any poem.

July 1968

The wild wind

Oh,
the wild wind
bending the trees,
crashing
round this house.

I love
The wild wind
when it cuts the ground,
whirls leaves around,
almost knocks me down.
I love
the sound, the sound.

I love
the sound of thunder,
storm clouds threatening,
grey skies darkening,
rain, relentless, obliterating.

I love
The ocean's storms,
the crashing waves that slash

the dangerous beach,
the rushing tide
the seagull's screech.

I love
wild days,
all their sounds and sights.
I love wild days
and I love
wild nights.

24 May 2006, 19 April 2010, 25 May 2022

Old tape machine

Which mode
Will you choose today?
Press PLAY.
Press PLAY.

And you will hear
my song of love.
Please stay
and make my day.

And now press REWIND
and you will find
my old love song,
still fresh as new.

I'm burnished
by the touch of time
and still I shine.
and still I shine.

Old tape machine,
old keys,
mechanically strong.
Electronics still switch on.

Old tape machine
Old songs of love.
I love you still
And always will.

14 September 2004

Love and loss

If your heart is broken
can you mend it?
And when you have to face the world
will it work to just pretend it?

July 2022

Love lost

He phoned
to enquire about his children.
That was all.
His wife
recorded in her diary,
"another nuisance call."

28 August 2002

Undercover Lovers

Lyric or poem?

1

They share a life of action
and a passionate attraction.
Secret agents. Secret lovers.
Life of danger. Dangerous lovers.
Keep their secrets under cover.
Love is better undercover.

2

She's Nadia Mayerkovski
when reporting to the Kremlin
but her name is Kate O'Connor
when she touches down in London.
Secret agent. Secret lover.
Keeps her love life under cover.

3

Wearing jewellery by Cartier
she joins the glitterati
at ministerial parties.
She's clever and she's smart, she is.
Will anyone discover
that she's working undercover?

4

He wears a dark suit and dark shades.
One of the Prime Minister's aides.
When the world's media gather
he's there at the elbow of power.
Will anyone discover
that he's working undercover?

5

They contrive a life above suspicion
because the purpose of her mission
must for ever be concealed.
So it's only undercover
with her lover, with her lover,
that the naked truth's revealed.

6

Their secret assignations
are vital to five Nations,
so they travel incognito,
and meet in Ravenna and Kyoto
and in Moscow and Vienna.
Crossing continents, double-crossing the world.

7

Here today and Bonn tomorrow.
Where next? He, Turkistan.

She, Spain. All part of the game.
A life of masks, a life of lies.
A life of action and deception
Such is the life of spies.

8
Is their love a true romance?
Or just a shot in the dark,
a game of chance, or an act,
a trick, a trap, or a plan of attack?
Take a chance and bight the bullet.
Love is dangerous, undercover.

9
Is it live and let die?
Where does the truth lie?
Is just one of them lying
or perhaps the other?
Love is dangerous undercover.
Never trust a spy.

10
Show no fear. Show no fear.
Coolly sip your vermouth
beneath the chandelier.
Observe the chattering
assassins hovering near.
But show no fear. Show no fear.

11

They share a life of action

and a passionate attraction.

Secret agents. Secret lovers.

Life of danger. Dangerous lovers.

Keep their secrets under cover.

Love's exciting undercover!

7 April 2001, 3 January 2013

As a song just a few of the verses might be selected. For example, 1, 5, 8, 9, 11.

Apple strudel
Verses for St Valentine's Day

My darling,
you are the apple strudel of my eye,
naughty but nice.

And yet,
friends warn me
that you are dangerous
and I'll live to regret
that we ever met.

I don't agree,
my delectable extrovert.
Time will tell our fortune
and I shall be
content to get
my just dessert.

6 February 2023

Lyrics

Come into my Kitchen

You look a little hungry.
I recognise that look.
I know what you're wanting.
You're wanting me to cook.

You look a little hungry.
Come into my kitchen.
Come in from the cold.
Maybe there's something you fancy.
Come closer to my stove.

You look a little hungry.
Come into my kitchen.
Don't hesitate to risk it.
I'm sure you'd like a little bun
or perhaps a suggestive biscuit.

You look a little hungry.
Come into my kitchen.
You could help me cook a meal.
Put something in my oven.
How does that appeal?

January 2019, May 2020

Jack

Must you go, Jack?
Yes, you must, Jack.
You betrayed my trust, Jack.

It was like a stab in the back, Jack.
Only worse than that, Jack.
You know what you've done.

Oh Jack, I used to love you,
couldn't stop thinking of you,
believed every loving word you said.
I believed you. I believed you.

You had your fun, Jack.
Didn't think twice, Jack.
There's no way back, Jack.

Don't try to wisecrack.
I don't want your feedback.
You know what you've done.

This isn't a game, Jack.
Things can never be the same, Jack.

Don't complain, Jack.

I want you gone, Jack.

No more chances, Jack.

None, Jack, none.

Oh Jack, this isn't easy.

I cry and grieve. I'm losing you.

Lies, lies, every loving word you said.

And I believed you. I believed you. I believed you.

25 February 2022

Wedding Song

This is our happy day.
Never thought such love
would ever come my way.

Feel like dancing.
Can't help smiling.
This is a happy day.

This is the time of times,
the best of times.
This is a happy day.

[Repeat verse one.]

This is a happy day.
This is a happy day.

Sing in a gospel style?

14 September 2017, 12.30 am. Palermo.

Big double bed

Oh
How I love
my big double bed.
Somewhere
to rest
my weary head.

Somewhere I dream
and dreams come true.

A place
I love
to be with you.

Oh
How I love
my big double bed,
my big double bed.
Oh, how I love
my big double bed.

16 August 2006

Antonio

Oh no, no, no!
Now you know
about Antonio!

I admit I've been a fool.
I didn't mean to cause you pain.
I can't make wrong right.
I think I was temporarily insane.

I guess I let my feelings
maybe disengage my brain.
I know I had so much to lose
and - so little - to gain.

But I suppose you know
I've always loved the dangers
of talking to strangers.
Playing it safe isn't for all
and if you take risks
you risk taking a fall.

Things can take a funny turn
when a cat's away from home –
all alone on a holiday,

all lonely in Rome.
In a bar in a café
I met Antonio.
How could I resist an alpha male,
an alpha Romeo?

Now I'm a little bit older
I'm a little bit bolder.
I thought, What can be the harm in
a man so charming?

Well now you know the truth
and I am safely home.
There'll be no more Antonio.
Antonio is gone.

So let's forget Antonio
What I've done, I've done.
There's nothing more to mention.
Antonio is gone.

There'll be no more Antonio.
No, no, no, no.
No more Antonio.
No, no, no.

17 March 2010

Trust in me

I've had several lovers
And for each my love was true,
But now I need a love to last forever
and I believe the one I need is you.

It's no life when love Is gone.
It's no life to live alone.
It's hard when no one loves you.
Where can you find a love that's true?

I believe that I can trust you.
You know it's time to settle down.
You've been around and tasted life,
and you've been broken-hearted too.

We could share a life together.
Trust in me and I will trust in you.
We could share a life together.
Trust in me and I will trust in you.

12 February 2004, 22 June 2017.

How could you know?

How could you know
what lies behind the show?

Oh yes,
I love the songs I sing
and all the cheer they bring,
but not everything is real.
You can't see the way I feel.

Don't be impressed
by all the applause.
It only seems
I'm someone the world adores.

Yes, it's true
men pursue me.
Why can't they see through me?
It seems that men are blind.

Honestly! What's in their mind?
Am I a tigress
that never tires?
Am I a star

that always shines?
Am a fire
that never dies?
Do you want the truth
or do you want lies?

When theatres
close their doors
and there is
no more applause
and audiences go home:
I'll be on my way
to another lonely town
alone.

9 February 2004

Let the bad times go

Forgive and forget
Let the bad times go.
There are better things to do.

After all you've been through
You need someone new.

I'll be
your shoulder to cry on.
I'll be
the one to rely on.

No more anger.
No more fear,
Darling,
now I'm here.

Forgive and forget
Let the bad times go.
Time to start anew.

Let the bad times go.

25 July 2006, 25 August 2016

Don't vanish with the dawn

We slept in peace
oh so close,
not knowing
the starlit world,
the stillness of the trees.

And the dawn
came soft and grey.
I touched you . . .
smiled,
like a child,
with stolen fruit,
half waking,
soft and warm
by my side.

Last night's wild love
in the sheets
still dreaming
of dark blossoms
reflected in the night.

And baby
it's warm here.

The daylight's cold.

Stay here my dream.

Don't vanish with the dawn.

22 June 1968

Julie Roberts wrote guitar music for this lyric. She recorded it in 2004 with Mike Piggott on violin and Gary Holder on double bass. Julie sang and played guitar.

It was released on the CD, *Don't Tell Me to Stop,* 2004. The words "soft and warm" are to be replaced by "strong and warm" when sung by a woman.

Afterword

My hope

I've always wanted myself, everyone I know and the whole world to be happy in love because people happy in love have the best thing in the world and, so long as their basic needs are met, are usually happy people. And happy people are good to deal with. They don't make trouble. They are nice to others. They want to make the world a better place. They don't start wars.

David Roberts worked in commerce for six years, was a teacher for twenty-four years, and has been a publisher for twenty-six years.

He is the editor of three popular anthologies of First World War poetry: *Minds at War, Poetry and Experience of the First World War; Out in the Dark, Poetry of the First World War in Context;* and *We Are The Dead, Poems of the Great War.*

His book of remembrance poems is *Remembrance Poems and Readings.*

He runs the publishing company, Saxon Books. Titles include *Falklands War Poetry, French Poems of the Great War,* translated by Ian Higgins, and *Cockerels and Vultures,* poems of the First World War by Albert-Paul Granier, translated by Ian Higgins.

He is interested in international relations and is an opponent of nuclear energy.

David is a music promoter, has a blog, *davidrobertsblog.com* - and a war poetry website - poetry of the First World War and modern war poetry by living service personnel, *warpoetry.uk.*

David Roberts lives with his wife in Sussex, UK.

Out in the Dark

Poetry of the First World War, in Context and with Basic Notes

Edited by David Roberts

The most important poems and poets of the First World War, and other poets of special interest, with women poets particularly well represented. The most celebrated poets – including Wilfred Owen, Siegfried Sassoon and Isaac Rosenberg – have been given whole chapters. Their work has been arranged in date order so that the development of their ideas and techniques may be appreciated.

Comments of past and present day critics, and basic explanatory notes on unusual expressions and vocabulary make this poignant anthology especially valuable for students. Extracts from poets' diaries and letters, historical and biographical notes, fascinating photographs and drawings give further insights into the lives, experience and thinking of the poets.

"I cannot recommend this book enough. . . I'm currently studying A Level English Literature & my teacher has actually used this book for reference. What else can I say, I think it's fantastic and is going to help my studies so much!" - Amazon Reviewer.

"I loved this book. . . This would be great if you need a book to help you with A levels or degree level, but it can still be enjoyed at a lower level or like me for general interest." from Amazon review by Hazel.

"By far the most useful anthology for students; it is really well designed, and gives students just the context they need for the poetry." — Felicity Currie, university lecturer, former assistant chief examiner in A level English Literature.

192 pages   9"x 6"   Paperback
ISBN 978-0-9528969-1-3   Saxon Books
For up-to-date information about price and availability see
warpoetry.uk

Minds at War
Poetry and Experience of the First World War
Edited by David Roberts

This groundbreaking and long established anthology of First World War poetry will appeal to people who wish to get to know both key poets and poems but also gain a deeper understanding of both the poetry and the mindsets of people caught up in the First World War. It includes the great classic poems of the war, poems by many women poets, and unfamiliar poems that are significant because they enjoyed huge popularity at the time they were written. Poems are set in their historical context, with many revealing insights from diaries, personal letters and accounts, pronouncements by the media, politicians and others.

This volume includes 250 poems by 80 poets, contemporary photographs and cartoons, maps, biographies, glossary and bibliography. *Minds at War* is an illuminating, fascinating, moving and comprehensive anthology of First World War poetry. It is widely used in academic institutions in Britain and America.

"My students are devouring it faster than I can assign readings. This is a great collection." – Thomas H Crofts, Assistant Professor of English, East Tenessee State University.

"*Minds at War* is no mere anthology but a comprehensive overview of the poetry and experience of the First World War. David Roberts sets the poems and the poets' lives within a contextual commentary which keeps the story of the war moving forward and provides as many useful historic insights as poetic." - Peter Carter, *The John Masefield Society Newsletter*.

410 pages 9"x 6" Paperback ISBN 978-0-9528969-0-6
Saxon Books warpoetry.uk

Falklands War Poetry
Poets from Britain, Argentina and the Falklands
Edited by David Roberts

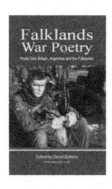

This collection of poetry about the 1982 Falklands war records the personal experiences and thoughts of servicemen who fought in that short but gruelling and important war. It also includes poetry describing the experience of wives of servicemen and the thoughts of a fourth-generation Falklands islander, Argentine soldiers and civilians.

The stories told in these personal poems and the views expressed are powerful, fascinating and moving.

These are the authentic voices of those who endured the privations and dangers or were closely involved.

130 pages   Hardback book   8"x 5" approx.

ISBN 978-0-952 8969-5-1

Saxon Books

To find out more about this and other books published by Saxon Books please visit www.warpoetry.uk

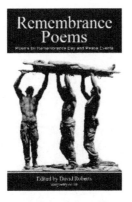

Remembrance Poems and Readings

For Remembrance Events and Reflection on Matters of War and Peace

Edited by David Roberts

Here is collection of words for remembrance events, and thoughts about remembrance, war and peace, spanning over two thousand years. Amongst these traditional, ancient and new poems, prayers and readings there may be found pieces suitable for twenty-first century Remembrance and Memorial events, and meetings or services that may focus on issues of war and peace. Some pieces may suggest ways of developing ideas for commemorative occasions.

A number of the pieces reflect on personal suffering and personal loss. Several poems are by contemporary servicemen.

Many of the items included in this collection will prove moving, thought provoking and even inspirational.

Paperback   120 pages   7.75"x 5" approx.

ISBN 978-0-9528969-1-3

Saxon Books

For up-to-date information about price and availability see

www.warpoetry.uk

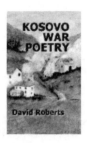

Kosovo War Poetry
by David Roberts

Kosovo is the Serbs' ancient homeland (as the 600-year-old Christian churches testify). In 1999 inter-ethnic violence broke out and NATO countries, in a clear act of aggression, bombed Serb civilian infrastructure and few military targets. This bombing inflicted massive and long-term economic damage and caused great social distress.

The poetry explores the human, military and philosophical dimensions. Includes the widely studied *Pilot's Testament*.

60 pages   Paperback   7" x 4.5"

ISBN 0952 8969 2 3

Saxon Books

For up-to-date information about price and availability of books published by Saxon Books please see

www.warpoetry.uk

ACRIMONIOUS

Printed in Great Britain
by Amazon

26506472R00076